What does an ideal monthly budget look like for me?

What are my financial priorities, and how do they shape my budget?

How do I currently allocate my income across different categories?

What percentage of my income do I want to save each month?

How can ensure my budget reflects my long-term financial goals?

What is my strategy for handling unexpected expenses.

How do I track whether I'm sticking to my budget?

What is one expense category I'd like to reduce this month?

How does creating a budget make me feel about my finances?

How can I make budgeting a habit that I can enjoy?

What tools or systems do I use to stay organized with my budget?

How do I ensure my budget allows room for fun and enjoyment?

What is my biggest challenge when it comes to sticking to a budget?

How do I plan for irregular or seasonal expenses in my budget?

What is my strategy for balancing fixed and variable expenses?

How do I handle overspending in a specific category?

What is my financial "why," and how does it guide my budget?

How do I adjust my budget when my income changes?

What are some non-financial benefits I've noticed from budgeting?

How do I involve family or partner in the budgeting process?

What is one way I can simplify my budget to make it easier to follow?

How do I stay flexible when unexpected opportunities or challenges arise?

What is the most satisfying part of successfully sticking to my budget?

How do I plan for future expenses like holidays or major purchases?

What small habit can I start today to improve my budgeting process?

How often do I review and revise my budget?

What motivates me to stay disciplined with my budget?

How do I balance short-term spending with long-term savings?

What financial goals have I achieved because of my budgeting efforts?

How do I use my budget to track progress towards debt repayment?

What are my biggest spending triggers and how can I budget around them?

How does budgeting help me feel more control of my finances?

What is my strategy for managing fluctuating income or expenses?

What rewards can I give myself for staying on track with my budget?

How do I incorporate giving or charitable donations into my budget?

What is the first thing I do when creating a new budget?

How do I balance needs, wants, and savings in my budget?

What has been the most significant impact of budgeting on my financial health?

How do I use my budget to stay aligned with my personal values?

What role does gratitude play in my budgeting journey?

How do I track recurring expenses to ensure they fit within my budget?

What steps can I take to make my budget more effective next month?

How do I approach budgeting for fun activities or hobbies?

What have I learned about my spending habits from sticking to a budget?

How does my budget support my long-term vision for financial security?

How do I stay motivated during months when budgeting feels difficult?

What is one budgeting mistake I've made and how did I learn from it?

How do I track the progress I've made since starting to budget?

What is one actionable step I can take today to improve my budgeting skills?

How does my budget reflect the life I want to create for myself?

www.ingramcontent.com/pod-product-compliance
Lightning Source LLC
LaVergne TN
LVHW082332200926
848481LV00012B/3325